Animals in the Grasslands

Written by Jo Windsor

Rigby

This giraffe
is in the
grasslands.

giraffe

This lion
is in the
grasslands.

lion

This ostrich
is in the
grasslands.

ostrich

This owl
is in the
grasslands.

This zebra
is in the
grasslands.

zebra

This lizard
is in the
grasslands, too.

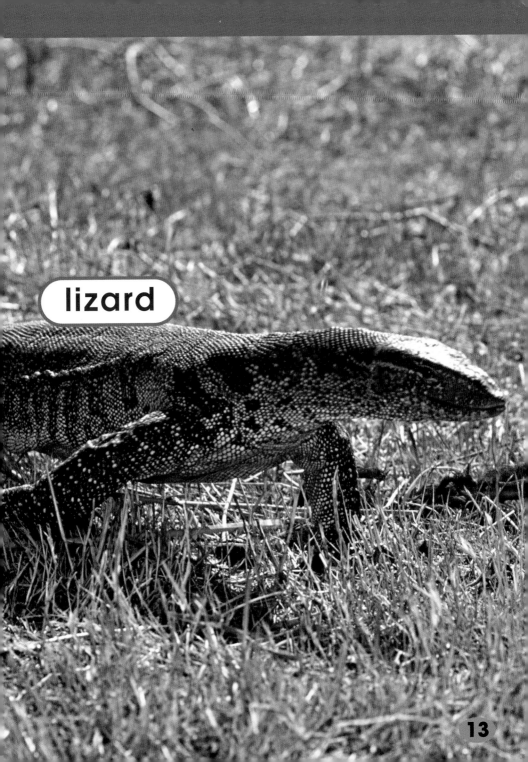

lizard

Index

▬▬ **Guide Notes**

Title: Animals in the Grasslands
Stage: Emergent – Magenta

Genre: Nonfiction (Expository)
Approach: Guided Reading
Processes: Thinking Critically, Exploring Language, Processing Information
Written and Visual Focus: Photographs (static images), Index, Labels
Word Count: 37

FORMING THE FOUNDATION

Tell the children that this book is about different animals that live in grassy places.
Talk to them about what is on the front cover. Read the title and the author.
Focus the children's attention on the index and talk about the animals that are in this book.
"Walk" through the book, focusing on the photographs and talk about the different animals and where they are.

Read the text together.

THINKING CRITICALLY

(sample questions)

After the reading
• Why do you think the animals live in the grasslands?
• Which animals do you think can hide easily? Why?

EXPLORING LANGUAGE

(sample questions)

Terminology
Title, cover, author, photographs

Vocabulary
Interest words: giraffe, grasslands, lion, ostrich, lizard
High-frequency words: this, is, in, the